ROMEY THE Homie

ROMEY STARTS KINDERGARTEN!

BY: DAWN NICOLE

Illustrations by:
Lauren Lacy

To my homie, Romey!
You inspire me to be greater
than I've ever imagined.
Thank you for showing me
my strength! You are the coolest kid
around & we're only going UP
from here son!

To infinity and beyond!

Love,
Mommy

Roman woke up bright and early, excited to start the day. It's such a SPECIAL day because it's his first day of school!

He got dressed!
Brushed his teeth!
Washed his face!
He even had a nice
healthy breakfast!

But as time went on, his mom noticed that he seemed a little down. While putting on his coat and book bag, she asked "Hey! Are you ok?"

Roman replied, "Mommy, I'm kind of scared. I've never been to kindergarten.
What if my teacher is mean? ...
What if the kids don't like me? ....
What if I get lost? ....
What if you forget to pick me up?! ...
What if they serve bologna?!?!
What if aliens come down from outer space and..."

"Whoooa whoa whooooa, slow down speed racer!" his mom interrupts.

"You're gonna love it!
I promise! ...
You're not to worry son!
You're not to worry!

Roman walked slowly to his classroom door, standing in between both his mom & dad as the door began to open.

"Hiii! Are you Roman?!?!" The nice lady exclaimed! "Come on in! We've been expecting you! I'm your new teacher, Ms. Asia!" she said as she reached for his hand.

Roman looks up and smiles, then takes her hand...

She showed him a coat rack that was decorated just for him! In big bold letters it read "ROMAN."
"You can put your things here! It's just for you!" Ms Asia said. His eyes lit up with excitement!
As she walked him over to where the other children were, she announced:

"Attention boys and girls! This is your new classmate, Roman!"
She turns to him and says
"Roman, can you tell the class 1 thing you'd like them all to know about you?"
He looks up, with a smile and says
"My friends call me Romey."
They all giggled and said

"Hiiiii Romey!!!"

As he went to sit with his new classmates, he noticed his parents were still at the door watching.
"Alright baby... we're gonna go now! Are you sure you're ok?" His mother called out to him.

Roman looks back at
her and says,
"You're not to worry Mom!
You're not to worry!"